RISING

RISING

Poems for America

———

Jane Beal

RESOURCE *Publications* • Eugene, Oregon

RISING
Poems for America

Copyright © 2015 Jane Beal. All rights reserved. Except for brief quotations in critical publications or reviews, no part of this book may be reproduced in any manner without prior written permission from the publisher. Write: Permissions, Wipf and Stock Publishers, 199 W. 8th Ave., Suite 3, Eugene, OR 97401.

Resource Publications
An Imprint of Wipf and Stock Publishers
199 W. 8th Ave., Suite 3
Eugene, OR 97401

www.wipfandstock.com

ISBN 13: 978-1-4982-2182-5

Manufactured in the U.S.A.   03/27/2015

For Stacey Lee Jones,

my friend since I was five years old,

whose name means *resurrection*

> "...As West and East
> in all flat maps (and I am one) are one,
> so death doth touch the resurrection."
>
> —John Donne,
> from "Hymne to God, my God, in my Sicknesse"

Contents

ACKNOWLEDGMENTS | ix

MAPS OF BEGINNING
LEGEND | 2
MAP READING | 3
THE BRIDGE OVER THE CANYON | 4

DREAMS OF GA-LUN-LA-TI
TWO HERONS IN AUGUST | 6
SKY-WOMAN REMEMBERS | 7
FIRST MAN SINGS TO FIRST WOMAN | 8
MY CHEROKEE CHILDHOOD | 9
USQUANIQDI | 10

SONGS OF WOMEN
DAUGHTERS OF AFRICA | 12
POCAHONTAS SINGS | 13
SOR JUANA INES DE LA CRUZ SINGS OF A SWAN | 15
A PRAYER OF MARTHA BALLARD, MIDWIFE | 17
SONG OF SOJOURNER TRUTH | 18

REVOLUTIONS OF DESIRE
MR. EMERSON EXPLAINS HIS SHOCKING BEHAVIOR | 28
EMILY INVERTED | 29
SONG OF MY SOUL | 30
MEASURING THE MISSISSIPPI | 46
STITCHING | 47

BIRDS OF LIGHT
GOD'S LIGHT | 50
THE BEGINNING OF SPRING | 51
A DOVE FLUTTERED DOWN | 52
GREAT WHITE EGRET | 53
FIELD MUSIC | 55

MUSIC OF THE WEST
SAXOPHONE IN F | 58
CALLIOPE IN CALIFORNIA | 60
WELCOMING AN INUIT CHILD | 61
A BENEDICTINE SISTER MAKES A MOSAIC | 63
MEXICAN WOODCARVER | 65
VALLEJO | 66
BLESSING THE MARMOT IN THE MORNING | 71

GHOSTS OF DAY
FIRST GHOST OF THE DAY | 74
SECOND GHOST | 75
GHOST OF AN AFTERNOON | 76
EPITAPH | 77
EXHORTATION FROM A GHOST | 78

ROOTS OF RISING
FILIA MAGISTRI IN THE MIDWEST | 80
DESCENDING INTO LOVE | 81
SECRET GUITAR | 84
LIFE IN WINTER | 86
SCAFFOLDING | 88

ABOUT THE POET | 89

ACKNOWLEDGMENTS

Thanks to editors Anthony Battaglia, et al., "Map Reading" appears in *The Flyover Country Review* (Spring 2014); thanks to professor and editor Dr. Hardy Jones, the five poem series called "Dreams of Ga-lun-la-ti" appears in *The Oklahoma Review* (Spring 2013).

Thanks to editor Nikia Cheney, "Song of Sojourner Truth" appears in the anthology, *Verse/Chorus: A Call and Response Anthology* (Grand Terrace, CA: Orange Monkey Press, 2014); "Emily Inverted" first appeared on Robert Lee Brewer's blog, *Poetic Asides*, was later printed in my poetry collection, *Made in the Image* (Lulu Press, 2009), and again appeared, thanks to editor Dr. Pradeep Chaswal, in *The Muse: An International Journal of Poetry* (2013); "Stitching" appears in my poetry collection, *The Roots of Apples* (Lulu Press, 2012).

Thanks to editor Jo Swinney, "God's Light" appears in the anthology, *Closer to God* (Scripture Union Press, 2013); "The Beginning of Spring," "A Dove Fluttered Down," and "Great White Egret" appear on my blog, *Birdwatcher's Diary* (birdwatchersdiary.wordpress.com); I have recorded "Beginning of Spring" and "Great White Egret" as Mp3s in *The Jazz Bird* project available at http://soundcloud.com/jane-beal; "Great White Egret" also appears in my *Spiritual Aviary for the Year* (Green Wall Press, 2014).

Thanks to the editors, "Saxophone in F" appears in *shufPoetry* (Spring 2013); thanks to editors Jan Tritten and Nancy Halseide, "Welcoming an Inuit Child" appears in *Midwifery Today* (Summer 2013); thanks to editor John Han, "A Benedictine Nun Makes a Mosaic" appears in *Integrité: A Faith and Learning Journal* (Fall 2013); it is also read aloud near the end of my sermon, "The Morning Star Rises in Your Hearts," available online at http://sanctuarypoet.net/LINKS; "Vallejo" first appeared as a voice recording on my CD/Mp3 collection, "Songs from the Secret Life," but it first appeared in print in *Pudding Magazine* (Spring 2014), the themed issue on urban experience, thanks to editor Connie Everett; thanks to editor Peter C. Leverich, "Blessing the Marmot in the Morning" appears in *Avocet: A Journal of Nature Poems* (Winter 2013).

Thanks to editor Brianna van Dyke, "Filia Magistri in the Midwest" appears in *Ruminate* (Winter 2010) under the title "My friend Franklin is a theologian" and in my poetry collection, *Butterflies*; thanks to editor Susan Troy, "Descending into Love" appears in *International Doula* (September 2014); thanks to editor Lori M. Cameron, "Secret Guitar" appears in *The Penwood Review* (Fall 2013); thanks to editor John Han, "Life in Winter" appears in *Cantos: A Literary and Arts Journal*.

I am thankful that I had the unexpected opportunity to teach the introductory survey to American literature at Colorado Christian University, which enabled me to work closely with the writers that inspired many poems in this collection, and to my students in that class.

I am thankful for my life-long friend Stacey, my goddaughters Reina, Reneé, and Sage Elizabeth, the Kerns and Daruna-Colón families, Franklin Harkins and especially Gary for their inspiration of specific poems in this collection. I am thankful to my mother and step-father for their support during the completion of this book and to my brother, saxophonist and composer, Andrew Beal, for his work on the musical version of "Great White Egret," which honors the memory of my friend, Jennifer Eve Franet. I am forever thankful to my Savior and Redeemer, Jesus, who makes all things possible. *Solo Dei Gloria.*

MAPS
OF
BEGINNING
—

LEGEND

I touch the map on the table gently,
curious about what it means,

trying to decipher the square-boxed legend
in its corner that should tell me how to read,

but the symbols are obscure code,
and the language seems foreign

like something I learned in childhood
but forgot.

Now my translating skills are as rusty
as a tin watering-can left out too long

in rainy weather
in a garden that was over-grown

—where roses, over-blown, twisted
through ivy covering gray stone—

and the mystery of the unreadable map
pains me as I look out the window

where the sunlight is nevertheless still shining
bright—and very clear.

MAP READING

I hold up the map.
I can't understand it—

its red lines and blue lines
like arteries and veins

of a mysterious body
about to give up her blood

as I lower my needle
to her flesh—

this compass
still searching for true north

while the map shudders
in my trembling hands

and a songbird hidden
in a bush by the gas station

sings about something
impossible.

THE BRIDGE OVER THE CANYON

There is a way back
even if the bridge is broken
over the canyon.

I may have to go
the long way around
or down—

clinging to the rocky sides,
finding invisible footholds,
balancing carefully between

courage and safety,
remembering to breathe
as desire brings me to the riverbank

knowing I must swim across
despite the deep currents
if I am ever to find you again.

DREAMS
OF
GA-LUN-LA-TI

—

TWO HERONS IN AUGUST

I turn
at the edge
of the lake—

two Great Blue
Herons swoop,
each around the other

                      in mid-air

til one flies
east, not far
from my face

while the other
goes west,
and settles

                      in the water

eyeing me
through the green pine
and the yellow grass

like Sky-Woman
fallen to earth
from Ga-lun-la-ti.

SKY-WOMAN REMEMBERS

I loved strawberries
before I knew why.

They were so red,
they caught my eye on the path

as I stormed away from First Man—
because he had made me so angry!

When I tasted them, they were so sweet,
they reminded me of his love.

I wanted him to taste them,
so he could remember mine.

When I forgot all my anger,
I knew my Father

had thrown them down
through the hole in the roots

of the Tree of Life that stands
in the middle of Ga-lun-la-ti—

and soon enough,
I conceived.

FIRST MAN SINGS TO FIRST WOMAN

Sky-Woman, beauty,
the light of the Tree of Life
still lingers on your skin—

you are the picture of peace and harmony
when I watch you putting berries in your basket,
your tear-dress untied and open

when you cradle our baby to your breast,
and the milk of life sweetens his tiny tongue
in the morning when you sing to him of Ga-lun-la-ti.

I remember that place! How strong-willed you were,
climbing into the branches of the forbidden tree
and then crawling into the roots.

I remember watching you as you fell
through the hole in the roots
toward the shining ball of water—

I remember Turtle Island rising up to catch you
as the birds brought you safely to his back
and suddenly, new life sprang up at your lightest touch!

Sky-Woman, beauty,
you are to me always new, always life—
and my love for you is endless.

MY CHEROKEE CHILDHOOD

By blood, I was bound to Cherokee sisterhood—
She Who Shall Rise Up cut first her finger and then mine,

and we pressed them together,
Cherokee-daughter to Cherokee-granddaughter

not knowing our mother was Sky-Woman
and the roots of our Tree of Life

grew down into our veins
from Ga-lun-la-ti.

USQUANIQDI

Miracle-child, Usquaniqdi,
your mother and her sister are calling your name!

We are wearing our tear-dresses now,
for we have walked that Trail.

You are so young, so we will sing to you
the stories we have hidden in our baskets.

We will teach you to plant strawberries
for your wife to find in your garden when you are grown.

We will kiss you in the light
that comes down from Ga-lun-la-ti!

For you are our treasured one,
the one the Great Spirit gave

when he breathed new life into you
with the scent of orange blossoms.

SONGS
OF
WOMEN

—

DAUGHTERS OF AFRICA

Mother Africa!
Seated on a stool,
wrapped in kenté cloth,
one baby on your back
and another at your breast,
with the whole African continent
framing your body
like a magical map:

I see your glory,
I enter into your story,
singing the names
of my twin goddaughters,
Akweley and Akuorkor!
Reina and Reneé,
the first a queen,
the second Reborn—

the hope of the future
that cannot be lost.

POCAHONTAS SINGS

I can't tell you my secret name. Only
my father names me by that name.
I can't show you how I ran naked before
I was eight or the deerskin skirt I had
at twelve. My turkey-feather winter-cloak
is gone like the sands of time dripping down
the hourglass you keep on your desk.

But I can show you the pot my mother made
with her own hands from the earth by the river
before my father, the Pohowtan, sent
her away to live with another man
in another village, and I never saw
her again. Remember, after you English
came to our shores, women pressed your cloth
into the clay pots to make new designs.

I am my mother's pot, my flesh is
her living clay, and you, John, have pressed your cloth
into my fabled skin and made me new,
as I, growing big-bellied with child,
lay dead fish in your corn fields to make them grow
for the boy I sing to when you call me
Rebecca, the noose who snared you, and I
call you Isaac when I hold you inside

my soul still turning cartwheels by tide
pools in Virginia, by rivers of water
frothing white over darkened waves where
the ocean meets Tenakomakah lands,

where the ocean from the east meets the river
from the west, north of Jamestown, where
your people first settled, and I fed them
corn and pumpkin seeds when they were dying.

The dying lived, and you came, and brought me
back to the King of England, who danced
with me at a masque as Ben Jonson's players
revealed a vision of delight, harmony,
and wonder, heralding a spring I will
never see with you, my John, my Isaac:
hold my hand in yours, my husband,
for it is enough that our child shall live.

SOR JUANA INES DE LA CRUZ SINGS OF A SWAN

First Portrait

When I was young, the painter came and painted me
beautiful, a book in one hand, my other hand turned out
as if waiting for You to take it and ask me to dance.

But all my secrets were simmering inside me
like spices—like cinnamon—or red pepper
ground to powder and ready to burn your mouth.

My desires were as sweet as a singing swan.

Second Portrait

I went away from the house where I was fostered
and took refuge in a monastery dedicated to Saint Jerome,
and he came again, that painter, and painted me:

sitting in my black and white habit, a wall of books
behind me, one open before me (not the Bible),
my beads wound round my body and dripping down

my shoulder, across my thigh, held in my hand,
but easy to ignore in comparison
to the oval portrait, like a shield of faith, upon my breast

showing an angel with rainbow wings flying above
someone kneeling, like Paul on the Damascus road, before
the Power that changes us in the middle of our life's path.

Little did I know! All that would be asked of me
by the Archbishop—my books, my music,
my scientific instruments—for answering Sor Filotea.

Yes, I confess, I said that a woman has as much
a right as a man to learn to read and write, and to do it
freely! But I was not free. I was bound by my vows.

So I surrendered all.

Third Portrait

The painter came again and painted me before I died,
one hand resting on the book of my own works, the other
holding the breviary (for life is brief), while wearing

my *escudo,* another oval painting upon my breast, this time showing a
woman, an angel, and a dove
descending from heaven and announcing that

the new life had come.

A PRAYER OF MARTHA BALLARD, MIDWIFE

When the stillborn child won't wake,
when the breath I breathe into him doesn't move him,
when his mother's blood is still pouring out,
and I have to make a choice—

Lord, have mercy.

When the morning light comes in the window,
when darkness flees before the dawn,
when I walk outside in the tender mist,
and tears gather in the well of my heart—

Lord, have mercy.

When I sleep and dream of heaven,
when I wake and go to the baby's funeral,
when I comfort his mother and then return home
only to receive word of a another woman in labor—

Lord, have mercy.

SONG OF SOJOURNER TRUTH

Growing Up

The Colonel thought he owned me
just because my mama and daddy were slaves.
His son thought so, too, and sold me
when I was nine for a flock of sheep
and a hundred dollars. That was back when
they called me Belle, and I spoke only Dutch.
The new man—calling himself Master Neely—
he raped me everyday and beat me
with a bundle of rods and sold me two years later
to a tavern keeper. He sold me when I was eleven years old.

The tavern keeper sold me to Dumont,
and Dumont seemed kinder. I met Robert,
a slave like me, on a neighboring farm,
and I loved him. But the man who called
himself Robert's Master, he said no, you cain't
marry that girl down the road—because he knew
he wouldn't own our children, Dumont would.
So he beat Robert good and hard for loving me,
and then, Robert died. He just up and died
from that beating and left me alone.

My daughter Diana came after her daddy died.
There she was in my arms, her sweet face,
her mouth milk-wet, her eyes like Robert's eyes
when I looked down into her soul, and I could hear
Robert laughing, like he was right there,
like an angel come down to look over my shoulder
at this little girl we made, and sometimes
I felt his hands on my waist again, more
than ghost-memory, and sometimes I smelled
his sweat from the field, the fire of desire in his bones.

Dumont came to me when the baby was still nursing,
and said I had to marry, marry Thomas, for Thomas
was Dumont's slave. Dumont saw I could
have babies and still work, and me and my babies
were strong. He wanted 'em for himself and his farm,
so that's how it happened. I married Thomas,
and we had five children, all belonging to the man
who called himself Master—that's what he thought was.
But the first with my new husband, my baby boy Thomas,
he died, right in my arms, the day he was born.

Glory, glory, hallelujah!
    The truth is marching on!

Finding Freedom

But Peter, Elizabeth, and Sophia, they lived.
My last three babies lived in those days when
the State of New York, they were going to emancipate
us all, and we'd be free. Well, freedom looks different
from my side, yes, it sure does. Dumont said
he would set me free a year before the day,
but he changed his mind, yes, he sure did, claiming
my injured hand stopped me from doing all
the work I should. All the work I should!
I spun him 100 pounds of wool and walked off.

All the work I should, please. I didn't run! I walked
because I knew I was free. He promised, and I was free.
I was forty years old, and I was free, so I took
my baby Sophie, and I walked off, down the road,
and stayed with the Van Wagners. When Dumont came
for me, they paid him, but I told 'em I was free. But
my children weren't, and when Dumont went back,
he sold my only living son, five years old,
to a slaver in Alabama. I took that to the courts,
the courts of justice, yes, I did, and we got my boy back.

But he was bruised. His face was cut, his back
was beat. When I saw his scars, I remembered
what Neely did to me when I was nine, and
I didn't weep. No tears. I told Peter, no cryin' now,
because by law, we are both free. So he went on
and grew up and took to sailing, sailing round
the world, and he sent me five letters, but
I only got three. One day, he was supposed to be
comin' in, and I went down to meet the *Nantucket*,
but he wasn't there. He wasn't there. My son,
my only living son, was gone like the sun in a storm.

But by this time I knew a Son no one could take away,
I knew him because I met him at the Van Wagners,
and that Son of God, that Jesus, he was with me
when my son went down into the water
with the whales and the fishes, with the fishes
and the whales, yes, Jesus was. I heard his voice
callin,' callin' me, and he gave me a new name
on June 1, 1843. *Sojourner Truth*, he called me!
That was my new name. I told my friends, "The Spirit
calls me, and I must go." Then I went out to preach.

Glory, glory, hallelujah!
    The truth is marching on!

Preaching Truth

I preached the end of slavery
everywhere I went, and many, many
heard me. In Massachusetts, in Ohio!
I met Olive Gilbert, and I told her my story,
and she wrote it all down in a book.
I couldn't read my own book! It was an English book!
But there were others that could. I didn't need to.
My bones knew my story, my blood-memory
knew it well. Then I bought my own house
for three-hundred dollars in Northhampton.

My own house, my own house, what a blessing—
but I was rarely in it because I was out
preaching! I preached to thousands of people
in hundreds of audiences, yes, I sure did.
My words changed those people. My words
opened their eyes to the truth. Yes, the truth!
Because it's true that men who call themselves
masters will rape a nine-year-old girl,
but Jesus will set them free. Yes, Jesus will
set them all free. He set me free! He can set you free, too.

On my wanderings, I met Frederick Douglas,
Harriet Beecher Stowe, and Susan B. Anthony.
I even met President Lincoln! Everywhere I went,
I was a black woman-preacher, and folks
couldn't believe it—some said I was a man.
So one day, I just opened my blouse and showed
them my breasts, the very same breasts that nursed Diana
when she was new-born, and then folks closed
their mouths. But I opened mine again and again,
for Jesus had put a coal of fire on my tongue,

and I had to preach! And now the war was on, the war
to end slavery, and I went recruiting black men
to fight for the Union Army. My grandson fought
in the 54th Massachusetts Regiment, fought to set
other men free, oh, and he did. I wrote a song
for those fighters, and they sing it today, called
"The Valiant Soldiers," sung to the tune
of the "Battle Hymn of the Republic." Yes,
glory, glory, hallelujah! The truth is marching on!
For we are going out of slavery into freedom's light.

Glory, glory, hallelujah!
    The truth is marching on!

Seeing Glory

After the war, we fought some more. We never
stopped fighting for more. I rode on streetcars,
no one could stop me, sitting or standing, just being
there, saying: segregation is wrong, segregation is wrong.
I tried to get the federal government to give
land grants to the freed slaves from the south,
yes, for seven years, I tried, even met President
Ulysses S. Grant, but it didn't happen. I tried
to vote in 1872, but I was turned away at the polls.
I knew I had the right, I knew I did. I went ahead

and preached freedom for slaves, rights for women,
reform in the prisons—oh, don't you know,
Jesus came to set the captives free!—and I told
that old Michigan State Legislature
they couldn't go on killing prisoners. Murder
is wrong! I preached them a sermon
like they had never heard one before. Didn't
they know Jesus came that we might have life
and have it to the full? Death tried to get me
many a time, but I saw the glory.

I was living in Harmonia outside of Battle Creek
in Michigan, and that was a good place—
a little harmony, a little sweet singing out there,
on the edge of a battlefield—and my daughter
Elizabeth was with me and my two grandsons.
I was getting old and suffering pain, and my face
was drawn with lines. So I knew heaven was coming,
coming to carry me home, and I was ready
to see Robert again, and baby-boy Thomas,
and all those black men who died fighting for freedom.

When the reporter from the *Battle Creek Eagle*
came to interview me, my eyes were still bright,
and my mind was still lively. But it was hard for me
to speak. When a preacher can't preach anymore,
it's time. I knew it was time. My sojourn,
like Abraham's, was coming to an end on this earth,
and I was glad, and I was ready. I wanted
to go on up and see Jesus, and hear those words
he said he would say: "Well done, good and faithful,"
because I knew I'd been faithful to the end.

Glory, glory, hallelujah!
    The truth is marching on!

REVOLUTIONS
OF
DESIRE
—

MR. EMERSON EXPLAINS HIS SHOCKING BEHAVIOR

I am not the only man
to have opened
his wife's coffin.

I used to walk to her grave, everyday,
and I wrote to her in my journal
as if she were still alive.

She was not alive,
but I was
not able to accept her death.

I could not accept myself,
or God, or the universe, or anything at all
as I had known it before.

I dreamed the world was an apple,
and I was floating
in universal ether

when an angel appeared and told me
to eat this dream-of-the-apple-world,
and I ate as one fearing.

How could I not? I opened
her coffin to see
that she was gone.

EMILY INVERTED

Because I could not stop for Life,
he did not stop for me;
our ships just passed each other by
on each day's open sea.

Always I was sailing onward,
so never had an hour
to hear what he would say to me
or fear his cross-bones power.

Sailing past the ancient harbors,
deaf to the mermaid's song,
I fought no monsters on the deep—
my voyage lasted long.

I mended nets, I gutted fish—
work was my prayer each day;
I could not rest, I could not stop
chasing the salt-wave's spray.

'Tis forty years since I began
to sail before the wind,
yet if I could, I know I would
begin my life again.

SONG OF MY SOUL

I.

I sing a song of my soul, an extraordinary world of memories and dreams,
    a shining orb reflecting the light of a single Star's glory in a darkened universe—
like a candle, flickering, held up in the window at night so that anyone looking in will see
the face of the one holding it illuminated.
My eyes are like mirrors set in front of mirrors that reflect within one another for eternity,
generation upon generation, link upon link of DNA—
like grains of sand, like stars that shine, like promises to the progenitor of my race,
from the present moment in a wilderness of mountains, in the shadow of the high places,
back into the past, back into a garden lush with ripe fruit but surrounded by no mud-brick wall ever built by human hands (even if the angels wield their swords, still flashing, at the invisible gate),
and forward, too, as if we all climbed inside a time machine together when we stood in-between the two mirrors.

Yes! I sing a song of my soul, quivering like a sparrow on a branch, on a pine tree in the West,
remembering a lilac that last bloomed in my backyard, and just being
a sparrow on its branch, the tender flowers drooping around me, sending their fragrance into the moist air,
waiting for the sun to set and all the fireflies to come out, flickering and shining as the sun set beyond a forgotten prairie,
the sound of the train rolling down the track as it cut across the town,

the night sounds comforting even when they hinted at something full of dread.
Something dreadful, something wicked this way comes, a monster in the dark, a snake awakening in fury—
the mirrors might shatter from the inside,
the glass may break on the face in the window and streak it with tears of blood.

Listen! I hear a lullaby. It is the song of my soul, for babies and their mothers,
for lovers, for people who are lost but want to be found,
for my brothers, for my sisters (whether they want it or not),
for women who are old in Africa, or anywhere, for women who are young,
for women who are accepted, for women who are rejected,
for women who need healing, for women who are healed, for women who are pretending to be healed,
for men who are old in America, or anywhere,
for men who are young but want to grow into manhood,
for men who are young but don't know how to grow into manhood,
for men who are tempted to love men or want to be women, and wear their clothes,
for women who wear men's clothes and want to kiss other women but still have babies,
for every abused child, for every assaulted child,
for every slave and prostitute, for everyone trafficked against their will,
for everyone forced into an abortion, for everyone who was aborted, or miscarried, or murdered as soon as they were born,
drowned in a barrel or plunged into a pail of slops and suffocated because she was a girl in China
or a Jew in Nazi Germany,
for all the midwives, for all the doctors and nurses, for the surgeons who cut open bellies with knives—when it's necessary, when it's not necessary,
for men who rape and don't confess, for men who lie, for my father, for his father,
for every Cherokee whoever drank too much whiskey or gin, remembering in their blood the Trail of Tears,
for their children and their children's children and their children's children's children, fire-water phoenixes:

for everyone.

II.

The stars are shining in the black vault of the heavens,
and I stand at a high point in the Sierras, looking up at those pinpricks
 of light—
diamonds that spilled out of God's jewelry box and scattered across the
 sky.
I cannot hold them in my hands, I cannot wear them on my fingers, I
 cannot hang them around my neck like a gift from Solomon to Sheba.
Nevertheless, they remind me of the One Star, who, shining on the golden
 orb of my soul,
claimed me for a light in the darkness to reflect the glory.

Wisdom is my dance master; wisdom dances with me like the most
 intimate lover,
caressing my face with his gentle hand, kissing my lips-like-cherries,
 sweeter than summer,
and giving me rubies as red as blood drawn from the center of my own
 heart and his,
blood that buys back what was stolen in the past, paying for it in the
 present, so that the future is changed forever.
The One Star shines on the blood, and it gleams in the light.
I bathe my feet in a river of blood, and I leave footprints of blood wherever
 I walk.
Follow the blood. The life is in the blood.
I will sing it again: *the life is in the blood.*

I quest for my mother's breast, I thirst for the milk, and for the land of
 milk and honey, the land of plenty, the land of no fear—
to be held in my mother's arms, unafraid that she will ever put me down
 or let me go,
to be loved, to be wanted, to be precious from the moment of my
 conception to the day of my birth to every hour that I breathed ever
 after—
to be considered worthy without having to prove my worth,
to be beautiful without being compared to others who are beautiful,
to be valued without being priced, sold, or bartered,

to be valued without being Snow White, lost in the woods, serving strangers, endangered by apples on days when the hunger gnaws from the inside like an illness,
to be adored, my eyes looking into her eyes, adoringly,
singing the song of my soul to the song in her soul,
our eyes reflecting in one another's, forever,
the one mirroring the other, kissing each other, her lips on my face, my little open mouth kissing her wherever I touched her—
my beloved mother, my only mother.

III.

I go down into myself, into the secret place that no one knows, except One—where, sometimes, it is still dark.
I break open my heart, like a pomegranate, and I eat my life
like one fearing, like one fearless,
like fear is my enemy—

like it does not matter that the King of Hell
sprang up like a tyrant from a hole in the ground before my feet when I was gathering flowers
and seized me against my will and said I must be the bride of suffering, lost in darkness forever,
wandering in a never-ending sorrow, watching others in pain pushing stones uphill,
or reaching for fruit that pulls away so that the hand never touches what the stomach desires,
or bending down to drink water that drains into cracks in the hard ground,
so that we thirst, we thirst, we thirst like those lost in a desert, and nothing can quench that thirst.
How, as a bride barely alive, I longed to be rescued!
O break this chain of death and set me free! O save me, save me! My prayers are whispers. Can anyone hear my words? Can anyone hear me?
I am breathless with running away, and even in my sleep, I am still running,
my feet helplessly moving, while my body lies still, frozen in fear, and I watch visions of horror

appear in mid-air, or in the walls of this shrinking prison, always closing in on me
like a beast ready to devour me, but without the witlessness of hunger to drive it,
only the maliciousness of a demon who delights in causing pain.
Looking for freedom, I find none, and as a slave for twelve years, I constantly wipe my tears and hide my fears,
and nothing, nothing, heals the screaming child inside me
as the warden watches me, and I pretend
my prison is a playground, my sorrow can be joy, I can be lifted up in the wind, the wind blowing through my hair, and laugh,
but the laughter rises to a shriek or fades, fades, until no one can hear it, not even me, listening beside the dark waters of a river in hell
that I look into without seeing my own unseeable reflection in it
because there is no light to show me who I am, and everything is distorted,
and more are coming, more shades made ghost by the agony of living above the ground.

They cross over on the boat, paying the ferryman for the courtesy of bringing them to this darkness,
for the security of knowing that they are in the place promised in their worst nightmares, rather than wretched and forever alone on the shore—
yes! We climb into the boat and bow our heads just to be welcomed by the King of Hell and the Queen of the Damned,
to be kissed by her cold lips and observed by her calculating eyes, never our mother, never our help,
who ate her own pomegranate seeds long ago, and sometimes will be here on her throne, and sometimes, will be gone to a world above, far away,
and never will she raise her voice against the deeds of the Tyrant, or the whipping of the lash,
to defend the innocent (are any of us innocent now?)
for her power is in passing the punishment from her shoulders to all her children,
so that we learn her wily ways of pleasing when we should run, of praising when we should cry out,
of dreaming that one day we will rise,
but our escape is cut off.

Escape is cut off.

IV.

Who will make a way where there is no way? Who will open the road into hell? Who can defeat the Evil One who stands over us with his iron scepter?
My questions are endless, but I live in the shadow-lands amazed at what, even in darkness, we can do when we try.

I hear a singing girl, and I take her hand, and skipping along the banks of the Acheron,
we tell the truth. We tell the truth, we tell the truth, we tell the truth, and sing what is inside
even if no one hears,
and I can remember things that no one else sees, I can feel what no one else feels, and so can she.
There are birds in hell—you wouldn't expect it, but they are there—and not all of them are harpies trying to tear out our eyes.
Some sing the sweetest songs you ever dreamed or ever hoped to hear, and the voice of those songs
carried high in the air, reach far into the farthest reaches of hell,
and the man pushing the stone uphill may pause,
and the man who hungers may forget the fruit he cannot touch every, starving day,
and the man who thirsts may feel as if a single drop of joy cools his tongue
because the singing enters the heart through the ears like the love of a real mother
who longs to hold us and comfort us and make our crying stop because her love is greater than our need.
In our songs are all the stories of our lives, above the ground and deep in the earth,
and sad or joyful, they are true, and the truth is what makes them as sweet as blackberries gathered from brambles and thorns—never mind if our hands are scratched—
because our hearts are, if only for a moment, made whole by hope of change, someday, a change

and a glorious procession, in which we are dressed in white and crowned with gold and standing with a shining pearl in the midst of our breasts.

Telling the truth, I long to hold my brothers' hands, and sweep my sisters into my embrace, and be the mother we do not have, and I tell the girl.
I tell her how my brothers and sisters and I have all defeated death.
Even trapped in this half-life, death's victory is not complete. Not yet, maybe not ever, I don't know, even if sometimes I long for him to come to me.
I know there is another life. Even then, I knew it.

V.

Even in hell, there is a place set apart for wanderers longing for solitude.
But it is uncertain if anyone can ever get there simply by wishing, though wishing is not a bad place to start.
I don't know how we found it, the singing girl and I, but we heard rumors, rumors muttered in hell and carried on bats' wings,
and when the not-birds brushed over us, claws passing through our hair, we shuddered, but we wondered,
and we started to look.

At first, there was just a glimmering in the distance, like a jewel at the bottom of a stream,
and I wanted to go near it. I wanted to draw closer. My heart beat harder and faster at the thought.
I wanted my friend to come with me, and sometimes, she did. Sometimes she sprinted ahead!
But she came back to my side. And then sometimes she drifted far behind, looking back, over her shoulder, at the way we had come.
I could understand that.
So sometimes I held her hand and dragged her forward—I was so curious about that glimmering light.
Hope, like a flame, kept flickering inside of me, invisible but giving off a steady heat.
It burned like a candle in the wind, but it did not go out.
Then my friend let go of my hand.

She let go of my hand, and told me she wanted to go back to the shores of the Acheron,
and I could not bear that, so I let her go.
And a shadow followed her.
I let the singing girl go because we knew enough about force in our lives without forcing each other to do anything.
The flame in my heart bowed low, and was almost extinguished in the wax,
for the wick was burnt black, and I could not tell how long my life would last.
I turned my eyes toward the glimmering in the gloam, and dragged my feet, each weary step, forward, not knowing where I was going.
I had ideas, and dreams, but these had cheated me before, and somehow I knew that I needed something bigger than I could possibly imagine.

I sat on the inner shore for a year.
I could see the Islands of the Blessed across the moat, Elysium as some called it, or Abraham's Heart, as others named it—
not that I could possibly fathom what those names meant.
Many times I got into an empty boat and approached a single island.
The boat knew where to go all by itself.
I would get out and stay on the nearest island for a day. I would read, and I would sing, and I would go back.
The warden was watching me. The King of Hell frowned. But I was paying less attention to their eyes and their mouths.
I was distracted by beauty, seeing it again as if for the first time, in awe, enchanted.
I wanted to live on the island.
One day, like a bird, I grew wings from my shoulder-blades, and I flew across the shimmering, glimmering water to live on the island of my dreams.
Many castles there were on the island, and in the castles, many people, coming and going, and talking and arguing about things they read in books.
So I read the books in the castles, and I talked with the people about the books, which were full of the wisdom of the ages.
There was no end to all of those books.
I noticed that some of those people were happy,

but others had darkness in their eyes, and looked back toward the shores of the outer hell with fear, and did not speak of how they came to be here.

There were so many mysteries.

Many of the people seemed lost, even though I had found them.

It was as if they came to Elysium without a map, and stayed without a plan, and went to sleep and still dreamed the dreams of horror and woke up screaming.

That happened to me, too.

But people were in awe of my wings. They didn't have them; when they came to the island, they came the hard way—by boat.

The people were always looking at my wings, white and shining like a swan's, and sometimes I thought they were the most important part of me.

I spread them wide so that the light in the place, the glimmering,

was caught in the dew-drops of the feathers so that they shone like a net of diamonds.

I did not fly very much, but I knew that I could, and that made a difference in how I felt.

Meanwhile, my heart complained bitterly about my wings, but I told my heart to be quiet.

After seven years, I grew weary of all this.

I was always carrying things that were too heavy for me in those castles: books stacked as a high as a mountain.

Kilimanjaro was cradled in my arms, and I kept trying to balance the stack, as it tottered back and forth, dangerously, almost capable of killing me in my half-life.

I didn't want to live like that. Or die like that. I had seen a vision, through a hole in our sky (which is only the underside of the earth), of a sweet baby girl being born, and I loved her, and I gave her my name.

I missed the singing girl, and my brothers and sisters who defeated death, even if they were in darkness,

so I went back to the shore. I took the boat because my wings felt too heavy.

I wrote a letter to my friend, and she wrote back, but she stayed on the shores of the Acheron.

I stayed on the inner shore that looks toward the Islands of the Blessed.

Then, one day, I heard a whisper in the air, a promise there, that I would take flight once more.

VI.

No eye has seen, no ear has heard, no heart has imagined what the One Star has in store for those who see by its light in the dark at night.
I never knew my wings were so strong! I never knew I could make a journey of a thousand miles!
For beyond the first island, there was another, with a field of wheat and a castle built of golden stone,
and the wind carried me there over the water.

It was even more beautiful than before!
The glimmering increased to true light, and my heart rejoiced, but my wings folded.
Who I had been was hidden from view.
The people in this castle did not see my wings, or know anything about my heart, and I had to work to stay there.
I worked in the castle kitchens, feeding the children, and many of them ate and were satisfied.
But I didn't mind the work because of the light—
and I met a man who played the harp like a messenger of God.
He was more beautiful to me than anyone I had ever known, and I could see him clearly because of the light.
His name was Orpheus.

Now it is as if a drop of water falls into a deep cistern:
two lovers, side by side, see it fall from the open mouth of the well above them, through the distant light from the loneliness of the yellow desert above,
into the pool of water before them, where they are hidden,
and the drop adds one more jewel to the water-treasure.
For they look into the water, and they see in it rubies and chests of gold, lost coins and a lamp like the one that held the Djinn, diamonds and darkness and more—
they see their own faint reflections, a man and a woman in the water,
who have waited for one another for a thousand years.

On the utmost bounds of night, there the dreams came to them, the one of the other,
and the promise of their love was a sweet, secret fragrance before they knew each other.
They are like water and stone, stone and water—water in a desert for one who is thirsty and stone for a foundation in a windstorm,
and their house is a Castle Called Beautiful.
But they have not built it yet.

Orpheus was his name, and he had wandered wide and far, in many of the deep, green places of the world,
and everywhere he went, he played his harp and sang,
so that every creature who could hear was enchanted by his melody, breathing life and hope into their hearts,
like a mother's love can when we are born.
My heart was ensnared in his invisible net of song, and I was bejeweled with shining gems from ancient seas
as those gentle bonds made me hold still before him—
I, for whom, ever before, stillness had been impossible in the face of fear.
But fear was no longer my master.
For the power that went out of him
went into me,
and I could breathe, and hear his breath, like a waterfall over a stone staircase in a wood growing in the perilous realm.
His love for me, given in the light, brought healing like a child finding a seashell in the sand who, holding it up to her ear, hears the truth about herself and the ocean at the same time.
We were both swimmers and dove deep into the waves.
How extraordinary to see, one day in a sanctuary, that he had wings as white as my own!
I never knew a man so pure.

VII.

But how to get free from that terrible, dark underworld?
I could still hear the King of Hell, and his warden, the Queen of the Damned and her servants,
hissing like snakes even as I worked to feed children in Elysium.
Sometimes that hissing terrified me.

Then there was the blood-contract of a pomegranate:
I don't remember eating the seeds, but they were in my belly, and I couldn't vomit them up.
Sometimes I left the Islands of the Blessed. Sometimes I went and stood, shaking and shivering,
in the black center of hell where lightening seemed to strike without warning, and lost souls, like brothers and sisters, cried out in pain.
The suffering of the damned! The hopeless suffering of these ones, who were dead, filled hell like a dark fog.
I wanted to depart, but I could not imagine leaving behind all of these lost ones.
So I went back and forth, always traveling, always wondering if there might be a way to climb up and escape.

Orpheus left the blessed islands to come and look for me. He left the safety of the center to discover the girl who made a home in the dark.
Where were her white wings?
He played a song, and all of hell fell under his spell.
He came like a hunter, but his arrow was peace, and those who could not endure the sound of joy
swooned in the deepest of sleeps, dreaming about something impossible.
They smiled in their sleep without knowing it, so that the agony faded from their faces for awhile.
And Orpheus bargained with the King of Hell for my life.

Give her to me! he said, and the deathless god, with his iron crown, gave to Orpheus his heart's desire.

VIII.

So we began a journey together out of hell, but ever the path was treacherous, and as he went ahead, I fell behind.
I called, but he did not hear me. It was as if his heart was closed. I wondered how long he had stumbled in darkness, looking to find me, singing me back to life but without losing his own despair.
I longed to touch him but could not. I longed to reach him, but his footsteps carried him far away.

I could hear the echo of the ocean and the dream of the desert and the
    wind through the trees as he played the golden harp,
a powerful music that broke into my silence and set my feet free, so that I
    danced upward, feeling hope I didn't know I could feel.
I began singing back to him, but my voice was faint. I felt powerless when
    he seemed so powerful.
Fear was still haunting me, the dark Power, a menacing Shadow.
My feet were cold on the rocks. Sometimes I was cut, and I bled, even
    when he was trying to lead us so carefully out of darkness.
He paid so much attention to the path.
I wanted him to touch me, and when we rested on our three-day journey,
    I dreamed that his hand passed through my body as if my body were
    spirit.
I was as insubstantial as air.
But love made me stronger.

IX.

It was not that he looked back—but that he looked away—and was lost
    to me.
The faint memory of his lyre lingered in the ears of my ears, the memory
of his face in the eyes of my eyes, that had been opened in darkness.
So I came into the upper world gasping for my first breath like a newborn
    baby—motherless, loverless, but alive.
He had vanished, but I was suddenly living in a new body, with flesh that
    could feel for the first time—a wondrous thing—like Galatea, but
    who had sculpted me?

Now my hands were open, and I had a new heart,
and I began to meet women who walked barefoot on the green earth, and
    they told me, when no one else was listening,
that they had been born again from the depths of the earth, like me,
(though I did not tell them about the manner of my rising),
women whose bellies were full of new life—
and they called me an angel, as if they saw my white wings,
    wings that were invisible in the daylight above the earth, but that
    glimmered in the night when I stayed with them as they labored to
    bring forth their children.

I caught their babies, as they turned into time—from the womb to the
    world in mere moments, like magic—
a miracle, and when the eyes of their babies opened for the first time, in
    faint light, beholding the mystery of beginning,
I was with them, hearing their tiny cries, watching their mouths move,
    soothing them with a touch and speaking their names with love.
There are so many secret moments that no one else saw.
But the babies saw them, and they remember, in a secret place inside.

X.

I saw the Star like a bird, enormous and shining, in a vision of pure truth,
and he spoke to me and said, as we flew through the darkness of space
    toward a blue-green earth hanging in the middle of the galaxy—
and his voice was like many waters!—
this is my world, and you are my midwife.

Then I journeyed to new islands, seeking to fulfill the Star-calling, but I
    quickly grew weary.
For a man under the influence of the dark Power cut out my heart and fed
    it to wandering crows.
How they delighted to drink my blood and feast on my flesh!
I paid a tenth of my new life in those days to the King of those islands,
and then I fled, even as sisters whispered to me that his crown had been
    stolen from another.

How I longed for my Orpheus in those days.
I called his name, but he did not come.
Where was my heart? Where was my heart?
My love, I longed for you with a never-ending longing. I longed for you
    with a longing beyond words.

Love is not short, forgetting is not long, but memory is as long as life.
    Memory is longing.
I longed to find my belonging in you, but there were greater wings,
    shining over me as I waited.
The waiting seemed like it would never end. Ten years. I could weave a
    shroud like Penelope,

but I knew you were alive. As soon as I set my hand to the loom, I was already unraveling any despair I had made.

I had two looms in those days, and on one I was weaving dark cloths to wrap around the dead,
—for an astonishing number of people were dying all around me, even as I tried to revive them—
and the other was empty.
I dreamed there would be a day, a deathless day, on which I would weave a white dress on my second loom,
one that could catch the light of the stars and shine in your eyes, if I ever saw you again, and bring you joy.
For I wanted to be happy.
Wasn't joy supposed to be a part of coming back from the dead?

IX.

I do not know what is happening in the middle of my life's journey.
For the path has turned me back again under the earth to call the names of the dead, those who live in the darkness, to awaken their hearts.
I enter the earth like you entered—alive!—and so strange it is to see all those who are ghost.
Maybe I will lead them upward. Maybe their feet will find hope.
I know the deathless god, and his Power is broken in me.
For I died, but now I live, and I have risen from death to victory.

Who will follow me now? The Pied Piper cannot compare to my flute. Its silver voice is Life.
The rats are drowned in the Acheron.
The lost look up like they could be found.
Something new is here, being made new, for behold, the Star makes all things new!

My life is renewed like an eagle's, soaring down into hell, and maybe some will recognize me, luminous Saint with white wings,
as I seize them in my claws and bear them aloft,
up and out of the darkness.
They will eat their hearts like one fearing and be born anew, their spirits take on flesh,

and the valley of dry bones from which they came will be watered with a fresh rain.
Look at me! Alcestis is my twin-soul. Talitha, that sweet girl, is in my little sister.
If you defy the deathless god of hell, I will call you my friend.

XII.

It hasn't happened yet, the happy ending you desire (and I desire), but have faith in the fire.
The fourth man is standing there like a Star. Not a hair on your head will burn.
You shall come forth like gold, nothing that you have will be taken from you, and instead of ash,
the incense of heaven will linger on you—beauty brought forth from pain.

MEASURING THE MISSISSIPPI

Mark twain—
two fathoms
deep:

the water is high enough
for a steamboat

and safe enough for
now, but any
lower

and we stop.

STITCHING

I do not think you are
Hester Prynne.

Your pearl
is a phoenix.

Your scarlet letter
is invisible.

There are secrets
inside of you

no one knows,
and songs no one hears.

The silence is
unbearable.

But I am still stitching
by the sea.

BIRDS
OF
LIGHT

—

GOD'S LIGHT

God's light is gold in the canyon,
bright on the river rushing
between dark pines like tall angels,
wings rustling green as wind mingles
the songs of heaven and earth
so the Steller's jay tingles,

hops on the rock, then looks up high,
hearing an invisible Word
shining, mid-air, shimmering
there, with hope, everlasting—
the heart's hunger to satisfy
even in winter, long before

spring.

THE BEGINNING OF SPRING

I pause on the edge
of a snowy field
and turn:

the black-capped chickadees
are flittering and twittering
in the bare branches of a bush—

flirting and falling in love
as if this cold February
had enflamed their blood.

It's the beginning of spring:
new life is opening.

II.

We sit down on the edge
of the fountain
with our feet in the water.

We hold hands and look
at one another
with hungry eyes.

A white bird at your right shoulder
twitters a message from heaven
into your soul.

It's the beginning of spring:
new life is opening.

A DOVE FLUTTERED DOWN

A dove fluttered down
from tree-branch to water's edge:

I saw her white, delicate wings
open in mid-air

her bird's feet briefly settle
on muddy ground

and her beak dip down to drink
in the afternoon light before

she felt my footfalls
as I came closer

walking on the roadway,
then around the fence

to go home over the greensward
between the field and the pond,

and she startled up from the water's edge
into the safety of her tree

watching me with careful wonder
until I passed by.

GREAT WHITE EGRET

for Sage

O ghost of startling beauty!
Great Egret, with your white breast
that flashes in the sky, before our eye:
you swoop in a swift half-circle
your wide-open wings braking against
invisible air, there,
before you curve in the other direction
making half of a figure eight, the symbol of eternity.

Now you stand, balanced momentarily
on top of a low fence
peering down before you disappear
from the street-view,
—we follow you—unable to resist
the invitation to a divine mystery:
beyond the hill of ivy, the air has borne you
to the shallow waters of the stream.

There you are hunting.

At dusk, near the end of day,
hunger drives you, and you wade
in dark waters, your long neck outstretched,
moving slowly in your slenderness,
your legs as black as your wings are white,
watching the way of the air around you,
watching the ripples in the water,
watching for tiny movements in the silent stream.

Your twin walks beside you,
your white wings reflected in the water.
The trees overshadow you both.
When you lift yourself into the air,
she disappears as if you were never there.
But when the trees and the tall grass
conceal you, when you have gone on
where our eyes cannot follow you

still, we know, you live.

FIELD MUSIC

I.

Wind flows through the faded, summer grass—
the sound of dry music plays.

Time is passing in an ancient world,
and I am alone in the wild.

A dirt track has widened here,
and I follow it with an open heart.

II.

A white-tailed hawk is soaring high—
a tiny kestrel passes swiftly by.

I noticed the first before the second,
though the smaller hawk was nearer

and shot past my shoulder to hang, mid-air,
above the green pond nestled between two hills.

What do you see that I cannot?
Is it only your hunger that drives you?

My hunger has brought me here, to watch you,
yearning for something unseen.

Sometimes the sorrow and the waiting of this life
are too much with me.

O, that comfort would come
from the Invisible One!

Light, like angel-wings, opens around me:
bright fire in the ancient hills.

III.

Sky-dancing spirits, messengers of blue-sky
and distant clouds and trees tops I have never seen,

my eyes are open, and I see!
My ears are open, and I hear.

You have entered my heart, like wind through my hair,
where the sound of ancient music plays on.

MUSIC
OF
THE WEST

—

SAXOPHONE IN F

First, the breath,
drawn in at the reed—

and then the long neck of the horn stretches out
and curves around,

down, toward the keys
depressed by the boy

on the bus whose long,
beautiful fingers were made

to play jazz, hip-hop, gospel, soul—
to make the souls of the saints

jump and jive and come alive,
to make the ears of their souls

buzz like bees,
hum with harmonies—

born in Africa, raised in America,
now playing like dreams

in the fields, in the churches
spilling into the streets of Harlem

crossing the country to California
where, see?, dreams really do come true—

funk, flamenco, country, rag-time
rock n' roll, rap, every kind of rhythm

comes surging through the bell of the horn as it
curves upward and around

WAILING LIKE MAD.

CALLIOPE IN CALIFORNIA

I have seen the heavy-headed poppies
swaying, orange, on hills made green by spring—

in the shadow of the giant redwood
on days when the condor soars overhead

and the ghost of the grizzly bear goes out
as if hunting for his long-lost body

for his bones, his jaws, his far-ranging claws
for his mate and their cubs and the safe, dark cave

where they lived long ago in California—
yes, I, Calliope, have breathed the scent of those poppies.

WELCOMING AN INUIT CHILD

For Austin

Take the long road toward the mountains,
turn left at the church, and again at the mailbox,
onto the dirt road covered with snow
that leads to the musical green house
secluded from the world:
here, a baby boy is born into the water,
wise-blood from heaven
flowing through his Inuit veins.

In the caul, he comes,
protected from drowning,
in the morning when the sun is rising,
but the full moon still shines
white, full and gorgeous
like the belly of a pregnant queen
reigning over the Rockies
and the dark-green pines of January.

His sister, sweet Caroline, the first duet
of the bassoonist and trombone player,
is watching as he slides into the midwives' hands
and then into his mother's arms,
the mother who cries from relief and joy
as his father looks on, happy and proud,
and these songs go into the doors of his ears,
this love into the halls of his soul.

II.

I go outside to post the sign on the door
that tells the world *he is here!*,
and his first visitors are three chickens
who have flown over the neighboring fence
from the farm of their Russian owners,
flapping short wings against stout bodies,
all excitedly asking if their eggs, given to the mama,
brought forth a strong baby.

Oh, yes, nine pounds and alert, I tell them,
as they crowd toward the door,
wanting to go in to see the newborn,
and I have to explain
that the inside of the house
is not for chickens,
but I promise to tell the family
that they knew, and they came.

I smile as I return to the birth-room,
for their intuitive knowing,
and Nature's power,
has touched my heart.
Soon, Grandma and Grandpa come, too,
and sweet Caroline runs to them,
and asks, her face glowing,
"Have you seen my baby yet?"

Yes, we have seen you, little babe, strong boy,
and planted your placenta in God's earth,
welcoming you with songs of love.

A BENEDICTINE SISTER MAKES A MOSAIC

First, I gather the stones.
I bend to find them—flat, white, and shining—
in the desert around Santa Fe.

After singing the psalms at Compline,
I kneel me down over an enormous rectangle and begin
to place one mystery beside another.

Transfigure me like a melody set in stone!

My breath-prayer stirs the dust. I wheeze
like an asthmatic as first Moses, then Elijah,
and now Jesus emerge from the sparkling sandstone.

My Moses has golden horns because Saint Jerome
found them in translation. My Elijah carries a scroll because
the Word of the Lord that came to him comes to me.

Transfigure me like a melody set in stone!

The three disciples sprawl in awe-struck wonder
at the white glory-cloud bursting above them: for in it is
Christ Pantokrator, Ruler of All, Sustainer of the World!

He stands in the mandorla as if he is being
born from the Virgin, white against a turquoise-blue placenta,
a brilliant door in the unbroken opening of life!

O, transfigure me like a melody set in stone!

A red lining I piece in, red for the blood
of his birth and his passion, red for his sacred heart hidden
under stones of praise and the rays of his magnificence.

But at his foot, I lay my rock of purple amethyst,
the twelfth stone of the heavenly Jerusalem, the one I sing
in the daily breviary, the one I sing with my soul.

O, transfigure me like a melody set in stone!

When it is done, my mosaic where heaven and earth meet,
I show it to the brothers who asked me to make it,
and they nod sagely before they lay it in the barn.

They cover it with a grey cloth, and the afternoon sun
shines on it through cracks in the roof sometimes,
but not even the old ox or the crippled donkeys can hear it singing:

Transfigure me like a melody set in stone!

I grow old remembering it, hidden there behind a manger.
My hair turns gray, my skin around my eyes and mouth wrinkles
like a dried-out sunflower pulled up from the ground.

But then a man like one of the lost magi stumbles
on the monastery in the desert. He even finds the barn,
where he trips, slips the gray shroud aside, and hears!

Transfigure me like a melody set in stone!

My Transfiguration! He says he must buy it, as if
he were the merchant who found a treasure, yes, he says he must
redeem this lost work of art for a new sanctuary.

Transfigure, yes, transfigure me like a melody, a melody
    set in the white sandstone of Santa Fe!

MEXICAN WOODCARVER

Carving *santos* in the corner of the woodshed,
silent in summertime, thinking
of San Francisco and his beautiful Lady,
the Poor Claras who followed in his footsteps,
and the birds who listened to his words—

Maria shaves away the wood to find
the shape of song, smooth under her fingers,
the holiness in the grain and the dark stain
of what used to be a tree, but now ever more will be
her memory made visible:

made in silence today,
shining in the sanctuary tomorrow.

VALLEJO

Cross-roads

Before there was a city,
there was a cross-roads:
the Miwok, Suisunes, and
Patwin passed by,
leaving their marks
above Blue Rock Springs.
But they did not stay.

The Mexican General,
Mariano Guadalupe Vallejo,
built the beginnings of the town
for his bride, Doña Benicia,
who came to him, seventeen
and pregnant, riding on a mule.
But she gave birth to all of their living
children somewhere miles away.

Even the General's horses
tried to escape his ships
when they sailed past the city-yet-to-be,
and only his white mare
survived the terrible drowning.
But she avoided the city shore
and swam to *la isla plano*
to pray for salvation.

When Mexico could not keep California faithful,
and America stole her

and her golden dowry away,
Mariano dreamed
his city would be called Eureka
and made the capitol.

But they called the city Vallejo,
and the General's dream disappeared in a single day.
Instead the Navy built a shipyard
across the water from the abandoned city
for sailors and ships and shipbuilders,
for workers and for war,
and some soldiers took root on Mare Island.

But others rioted in the young
streets of Vallejo,
surprised to be alive.

Fighting

My family did not come intending to stay
in that Victorian house
on York Street.
We rented; we did not buy;
we planted no gardens.
The weeds in the backyard grew high.
We stayed there for years
without flowers.

There were children instead
—we started with nine—
and grew to fourteen,
losing four in-between (like Benicia),
and our General, my father, did brave things
that inspired us beyond belief.
He knew how to fight
the darkness.

He rescued a kitten from the top
of a telephone pole,

and I helped him
by steadying Jacob's extension ladder
under his courageous feet
as he climbed into heaven.
He came back down
soon enough.

My brother was jumped for his hat
the summer our city had the highest
murder rate per capita in California,
and one of our neighbors
died of alcohol poisoning—
another was raped.
I can still hear her
screaming.

Jim Maldinado, the tall-basketball-hoop man,
broke into our house after
he had moved out
and stole all of my mother's amethyst jewelry;
Mario, who went to prison for murder,
stole all the fire-arms,
but my brother got them back.
Only one semi-automatic hand-gun was missing a clip.

We opened the newspaper
and read one day of a city resident
who heard voices telling her
to drop her baby into the marina—
and she did it.
Her baby couldn't swim
to Mare Island.

Later, I collected flowers that grew
out of the cement cracks in the sidewalk,
pressed and dried them
with my Filipino girl-friends at the library,
and ate panzit and lumpia at school by day
while listening to Pablo sing in Spanish by night.

I still have those pressed-down, faintly fragrant memories;
I can still hear those Spanish love songs.

New Jerusalem

I left, but I came back
a thousand times.
Vallejo, the cross-roads city,
where there was more fighting
than oxygen,
became my hostile home for good,
for life, for some reason.
I grew up in that city.

When I was fifteen,
I became an optician
and a college student
at the same time,
but I was so tired one night
that I forgot to go to my art class.
My father was proud of me
for working so hard.

On Saturdays, I pretended
to teach English
to Spanish-speaking women
like Ofelia, who, at eighty, called me
muñeca—porcelain doll—
and pinned a gold angel on my collar
to protect me.
I loved her.

For a year of Sundays, I taught
little children at the local Church on the Hill
who told me how they survived
falling out of windows and boats,
how they recovered
from asthma attacks or metal bars

jammed in their sides.
I listened to the stories of so many childhood traumas.

One girl visited her parents in prison,
and another told me she was lucky
because she got to sprinkle the water
on her mother's coffin,
and I wondered how
the children of Vallejo could live.
Sometimes Vallejo was like
a New Jerusalem:

Talitha, cumi!

BLESSING THE MARMOT IN THE MORNING

I bless you, marmot, washing your sweet face
with your spit and your paws
by a giant gray stone
in the pine-tree shade.

I bless you as you scamper
through the tufted grass
and little yellow flowers
that grow in the Sierras in July.

I bless you as you notice me
noticing you; I bless your babies
asleep in the hole
you dug for them.

I bless you, marmot.
You remind me of God.

GHOSTS
OF
DAY

—

FIRST GHOST OF THE DAY

The ghost of a green hummingbird
flittered, twittered, and spun
on the arc of a dazzling sun-ray,
high in the sky—
but the purple flowers were calling his name.

Down he descended like Persephone
gathered by the god into hell.
His journey was through the darkness.
His eyes were closed,
always reliving the moment of his death.

The memory is a whisper inside of me:
I embrace the possibility of flight after death.

SECOND GHOST

The skin of the pomegranate is split open.
The seeds inside are showing through, wine-red.
When will we taste their sweetness?
How long will we have to stay to pay for this bliss?
My fingers can't help touching you.
I want to know what is inside.
The guilt is not unbearable,
no matter what Sisyphus may say.

GHOST OF AN AFTERNOON

The light is shining on the water.
The fat man has a little dog the color of copper.
A madwoman's daughter buys chocolate lollipops.
She puts them in a blue coat-pocket.

There are still some green trees
in between ones with red leaves.
The wind blows, and the leaves fall down.
Yes, ashes, ashes, we all fall down.

Orpheus sings, but Eurydice does not rise.
I see her running away in Elysium.
She looks back over her shoulder, all white,
as if she is afraid. Her hair is flying.

These ghosts are everywhere.
The light shines through them.
When darkness comes, they cannot hide,
but press into the flesh and blood all around them.

Flesh and blood turn cold as stone in winter.
Winter is rising.

EPITAPH

The harp twangs.
A string breaks.
The songs of olden times
go unsung at sunset,
unremembered in the dark.

EXHORTATION FROM A GHOST

Now name the thing you love,
and banish the impossible fear.

ROOTS
OF
RISING

—

FILIA MAGISTRI IN THE MIDWEST

My friend Franklin is a theologian.
With care, he studies representations
of Moses in St. Thomas Aquinas,
devout Victorines in medieval France,
Peter Abelard's florid *Sentences,*
and abbreviations like *Filia
magistri*, the daughter of the Master,
(which sounds like a person but is really
a book), and I am listening to him

but I am also looking beyond him
out the window at a tree with new leaves,
green and trembling on the branch in the wind,
as the rain falls from the gray skies and drips
from the leaf-edges to the soil and the roots.

DESCENDING INTO LOVE

First water, then muscles, tensing—
a message to your mother
that your journey was beginning.

The snowstorm had ceased,
the moon was full,
and it was morning.

We made our way to the birth-place
and looked out the window:
the Rocky Mountains were shining in the west.

As we waited for you,
your brother built a snowman
and sent us a message that made us laugh!

Your father brought food,
but your mother did not eat it—
she stood and swayed and danced.

Time was passing,
things were changing,
and you were coming closer.

Into the water your mother went
breathing deeply, her belly floating
as the time of birth drew near.

The pain grew greater,
but we trusted that you would turn,
rocking you with the rebozo in the light.

Then we lay down to rest, even though
not all the pain was gone,
and we listened to your heart.

We heard the moment when you
turned inside, your back now against
the curve of your mother's belly—

it was time! The gift time gave
was your life descending into love
as your doula told a story:

*once upon a time, I went zip-lining
over the St. Helena Cloud Rain Forest
in Costa Rica, and curiously*

*there was a blind man
climbing the stairs and riding the ropes
high above the rain forest!*

*I was afraid, but he was not,
and he took each leap of faith
fearlessly trusting he would find*

*the way down into the lower world
and love the way, and love the way!,
and led him home at last.*

Women came and went,
talking of this and that,
but you were ready to emerge.

With strength and courage,
your mother moved you
from the womb toward the world,

saying, "I feel her fingers!"
and here, you came with your right hand
reaching out to touch this life

like an artist reaches out
toward canvas or clay,
like a gentle healer reaches out

to touch the hurting
and bring them help—
so you were helped

as your midwife
brought her hands to your head
and turned you into time.

So you were born, beautifully,
purple as your name, then pink—
and hardly cried, comforted by your mother.

Sweet baby girl! Welcome to the world—
may your life be ever blessed.

SECRET GUITAR

Amish boy raised
in silence,
occasionally broken
by the Vaterunser,
hides a secret guitar
in the haystack,
his forbidden music
beyond the wheat field.

But a pitchfork in the hay
snaps the guitar's neck,
and when wrenched out
in surprise
by Father Farmer,
scissors apart
the taut, gut strings—
twanging, but oddly, in tune.

Then the horse in the barn discovers
the boy's dangerous accordion
in the manger,
chews the bellows
of the squeezebox
with big, yellow teeth,
rolling wild eyes
at the taste of splinters
and the happy sound
of a forgotten polka.

Hearing the pitchfork-song
from the field harmonize
with the horse's ballad
from the barn,
the boy stifles
laughter and tears, wondering
how the blues harp in his shirt-pocket
will sound under the moon.

At dusk, walking up
to the next farm,
he peers into an open window
and sees a six-year-old girl
penciling black and white keys
onto an old piece of cardboard,
then closing her eyes to play
her silent piano to God.

LIFE IN WINTER

There is a green tree
on the street around the corner—

all the other trees
stretch out bare branches

but this one, miraculously,
has hardy, green leaves

and snowfall after snowfall,
it is still shining

so that I marvel!

Are the roots, somehow,
keeping warm underground?

Do they drink from a secret stream
that flows only to them?

How is it that when all the other trees
have died and are waiting to be born again

in a far-off springtime
that can hardly be imagined

this tree is still alive?

Sweet Jesus, give me the secret
hidden in those branches

enclosed in that bark—
an invisible but still vital sap

because I want blood like that
to ooze slowly through my veins

as I cross over from the old year to the new
to witness Epiphany

and bow down knowing
I was born to live and never die.

SCAFFOLDING

Fragile scaffolding of the soul—
I feel like a child

excited to climb up
who suddenly looks

down.

The ground is so far away,
there are clouds beneath my feet.

But the stars above
are almost in

reach.

ABOUT THE POET

Dr. Jane Beal is a poet. She was born and raised in northern California, where she received her BA (Sonoma State University), MA (Sonoma State University), and PhD (UC Davis) in English literature with concentrations in medieval literature, classical mythology, and the literature of the Bible. She has served as a professor at Wheaton College and Colorado Christian University, teaching literature and creative writing, and as a midwife in the U.S., Uganda, and the Philippine Islands. She currently teaches at the University of California, Davis.

In addition to *Rising: Poems for America*, Jane is the author of other poetry collections, including *Sanctuary* (Finishing Line Press, 2008) and several more published by Lulu Press: *Made in the Image, Magical Poems, Tidepools, Love-Song, Butterflies, Epiphany: Birth Poems, A Pure Heart, Sunflower Songs* and *The Roots of Apples* as well as her Birdwatcher Trilogy, *The Bird-Watcher's Diary Entries, Wild Birdsong* and *Jazz Birding*. She has made three recording projects, *Songs from the Secret Life, Love-Song*, and, with her brother, saxophonist and composer Andrew Beal, *The Jazz Bird*. She also writes fiction, creative non-fiction, and works of literary scholarship.

To learn more, visit sanctuarypoet.net.

A barn swallow swooped up,
dancing on the wind,
darting,
split-tailed,
a spirit of pure joy!

jb

www.ingramcontent.com/pod-product-compliance
Lightning Source LLC
Chambersburg PA
CBHW060420090426
42734CB00011B/2384